The Niche Trading System

Binary Options Basics and Trading Plan

D1827512

Brian Petro

Contents

Introduction

To start off, it is important to understand that before commencing your trading career, trading is easy. But trading is not your goal. In order to make money trading you need to learn to trade well. This strategy guide will teach you a niche strategy in order to help you reap larger profits as you begin to trade, but it will not give you every skill necessary to turn trading into your career. With that said, be aware that all investments carry risk and you should only start with the amount of money you are willing and able to loose.

Fortunately, the techniques I am about to teach you will come in handy even for the traders with the smallest size investment. Although later the risk management strategy will help you understand why you may potentially want to start with a higher initial balance, it is still very feasible to begin trading with even less than $500.

Reason for Writing

Over the years that I have been involved in the markets I have come to realize that a major aspect of remaining successful is being able to stick with a winning plan. Using this reasoning, I decided it would be mutually beneficial to me as well as fellow traders to write a detailed strategy book describing the methods used to make money in this niche market. This way I can become more familiar with my own strategies while creating material for a field of trading that has very little literature.

Importance of a Trading Plan

"Without a plan, you are planning to fail."

It is important to realize that throughout this trading system I am going to outline more than one way to make profits with binary options. Another important fact I have learned in life is that the best way to follow a plan and be successful is to have it all written out. That is why I encourage you to work on creating your own plan while studying this strategy. This way when you start to trade you will have already made yourself the most familiar with the trading options that fit you best. To help facilitate this, I have included a copy of the trading plan I used when starting to trade binary options.

Furthermore, I have gone through the plan and highlighted the sections I feel are most important for traders to tailor to their personal trading style. Completing your own version of the trading plan, as well as sticking to it, may be the most important variable in making you a successful trader.

Analyzing Charts

Learning Technical Analysis

Technical analysis is an essential weapon in the arsenal of anyone finding their place in financial markets. Learning the technical analysis of charts is a guaranteed prerequisite to anyone's trading career. Fortunately, technical analysis can be learned fairly quickly. There are a plethora of books that teach technical analysis of charts using different styles, mainly consisting of candle sticks (see the titles at the end of this section for suggested reading, as well as the links at TradeTheNiche.com). At least one book on technical analysis should be studied before attempting any type of trading in the financial markets. This section will give a brief overview of technical analysis, but this book is devoted to teaching a successful binary option strategy, not teaching the basics of trading in the markets. At the end of the section I will also include resources to further your technical analysis education.

Understanding Market Moves

Understanding the essentials of what makes the market moves is necessary in order to be successful in the trading world.

Psychology is a well-known derivative of most moves in the financial markets. Unfortunately, in order to understand this psychology it becomes increasingly more important to be up to date with the methods that the masses use in order to make trading decisions; for example, knowing candlestick analysis.

Using different technical analysis methods it is possible to increase your chance of making a winning trade. Although technical analysis cannot predict the actual movements of a given instrument, it can help you understand how other traders view it. This is actually more important than knowing what a financial instrument should do, considering the real price in determined by what people will actually pay for it.

Another factor in determining market moves is the news. Being able to determine the effects of market news on the market is only one part in determining the overall psychology of a financial instrument, but can also be one of the most important. Before any trade, it is highly suggested that you check any related news for that instrument. It is not uncommon for all indicators to look like a stock is going one way, and then one bad news story sends it the other way. Avoiding this mistake is as easy as doing a quick internet search and can potentially save you thousands in losses.

Candle Stick Patterns are unquestionably one of the most reliable and easy to learn indicators that any trader can use. Candle Stick Patterns can have one of the biggest effects on the psychology of the markets; therefore it is an essential tool in your trading arsenal. There are also other technical indicators that can be easily learned and would be very beneficial to the accuracy of your speculation. Some of the most popular indicators are volume bars, moving average lines, Bollinger bands, stochastic indicators, and Fibonacci indicators; all which will help your understanding of the overall market psychology. Most of these indicators can be easily explained and are readily available on most popular charting systems.

If you decide to make trades over periods longer than a week, which is unusual for binary options, than it would also be a good idea to check the fundamental analysis of the financial instrument. This would mean checking the countries financial reports when trading currency pairs and researching indicators like the P/E ratio and insider trading statistics when speculating on stocks.

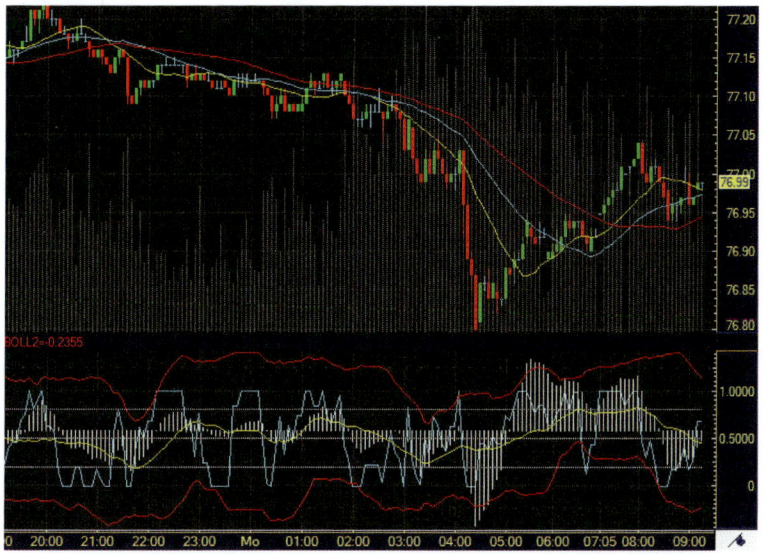

Here is an example of a chart with multiple technical indicators.

Useful Books for Technical Chart Reading

Technical Analysis of the Financial Markets: A Comprehensive Guide to Trading Methods and Applications (New York Institute of Finance) by John J. Murphy

Japanese Candlestick Charting Techniques, Second Edition by Steve Nison

The Universal Principles of Successful Trading: Essential Knowledge for All Traders in All Markets (Wiley Trading) by Brent Penfold

Getting Started in Candlestick Charting by Tina Logan (May 2, 2008)

Encyclopedia of Candlestick Charts (Wiley Trading) by Thomas N. Bulkowski

Useful Links for Technical Analysis

http://tradetheniche.com/technicalResources.html - Our Page of Technical Resources

http://premium.working-money.com/wm/display.asp?art=481 – Candlesticks and Trend Lines

http://stockcharts.com/school/doku.php?id=chart_school – Technical Analysis School

http://stockcharts.com/school/doku.php?id=chart_school:chart_analysis:candlestick_pattern_ - Candle Stick Dictionary

http://www.investopedia.com/active.asp#axzz1ViVxXNb9 – Technical Analysis Tools

Real Time Data

The real-time data stream you acquire will be like the back bone of your entire operation. Without accurate knowledge of what is happening real time in the trading world, it will be very hard to become a trader. Most binary options brokers allow you to trade many different types of instruments. These include, but are not limited to, foreign currency, stock indices, oil, gold, silver and even corn. In order to begin trading any of these it is important to have real-time data of the underlying indicator. This means if you plan trading currency options you are going to want to have real-time data for currencies. If you were interested in stock indices it would be important to have a subscription to real-time data for those indices, and so on.

The smaller the time frame you decide to work on, the more important having real-time data becomes. Many binary brokers have options that expire every hour, and some even faster than that. For the trader this means two very different things. The first is that it means the trader has the option to make profits more often than almost any other type of trading. The second is that on these short time frames, the reliability and access to up to date information becomes increasingly more important.

Getting Real-Time Data

There are many places online where you can get access to real-time data. At the end of this section I will include a few links to sites I recommend. To start off, the most important thing to consider before purchasing your data feed is what instrument you are going to trade. For example, if you are going to trade currencies only, you only need a currency feed. But if you plan on trading commodity futures, you will want to get a futures exchange feed.

Personally, I recommend starting with currencies. Currencies also happen to be one of the cheapest real-time data feeds to get. Furthermore, they are traded all day long and do not stop when the markets close. This way you can better watch your instrument of choice. There are also many more resources to help you predict each currency pair since there are only a limited number.

Esignal - www.esignal.com/OnDemand - This is an elite charting package customizable for many types of users, also they have great customer service.

*A quick tip to get free software, especially for forex, would be to sign up for a forex brokerage account with someone like eToro USA. They have a fairly low minimum balance. There are also many others that do the same type of deals, search around to find one that fits you best.

Setting Up Your Trading Platform

Fortunately, not many skills go in to knowing the platform when trading binary options. This way all energy can be focused on making high probability trades. In this section I will explain the process of signing up and getting started in your binary options account.

Nadex

The North American Derivatives Exchange is my personal choice when it comes to trading binary derivatives. To start off, they are one of the few regulated exchanges. Another important reason this platform excels is that it allows you to exit positions before the expiration date, as well as bet on multiple contracts involving the same instrument. These are both essential in order to hedge your trades.

To join the Nadex go to www.nadex.com. Click on the "Join Exchange" button and sign up for an account. You can start trading with as little as $100, but remember, it will be much easier to take in consistent low risk profits with a higher account balance than it would be to make large profits with a small account balance. As long as you can convince yourself to only trade with one contract per position, I would suggest a starting balance closer to $500.

Once you are registered with Nadex, you can log in and will be taken to the browser based trading platform. I suggest you make yourself familiar with the set up before you begin trading; on the next page I have included some pictures with details to help you.

When trading on Nadex, I suggest you stay away from the "Bull Spreads." They have very big spreads and are quite hard to actually profit from.

Markets	Page 1 of 2		Display	View as List	
EUR/USD >1.4560 (3PM)	25-AUG-11	250	0.50	3.00	250	09:45:36
EUR/USD >1.4540 (3PM)	25-AUG-11	250	2.00	5.00	250	09:45:53
EUR/USD >1.4520 (3PM)	25-AUG-11	250	6.00	8.50	250	09:45:52
EUR/USD >1.4500 (3PM)	25-AUG-11	250	11.50	15.00	250	09:45:53
EUR/USD >1.4480 (3PM)	25-AUG-11	250	20.00	24.00	250	09:45:53
EUR/USD >1.4460 (3PM)	25-AUG-11	250	31.50	36.00	250	09:45:52
EUR/USD >1.4440 (3PM)	25-AUG-11	250	44.50	49.50	250	09:45:53
EUR/USD >1.4420 (3PM)	25-AUG-11	250	58.50	63.00	250	09:45:53
EUR/USD >1.4400 (3PM)	25-AUG-11	250	71.00	75.00	250	09:45:54
EUR/USD >1.4380 (3PM)	25-AUG-11	250	81.50	85.00	250	09:45:53
EUR/USD >1.4360 (3PM)	25-AUG-11	250	89.00	92.00	250	09:45:53

Here is an example wide variety of instruments you have to trade. These are all designed around the EUR/USD currency pair. Each underlying instrument, such as currency pairs, has a list of binary options like this. All other underlying instruments, such as indices and commodities, have lists of binary options as well. On the left, a description tells you the underlying instrument (Red), the strike price(Blue), and the time in which the option expires (Green).

Risk Management

Why Risk Management

Through years of experience, if I had to give one piece of advice about the markets, I would say to be successful you need to have a sound risk management strategy. Many people spend months, if not years, learning technical and fundamental analysis in order to enter their dream job of trading. It sounds so simple, "If I just learn all of the indicators and I'll soon be off to making millions in the comfort of my own home. Wrong. It doesn't matter if you can just read candle sticks or know every advanced technical indicator ever created by man, without a sound risk management strategy you are doomed to fail before you ever make your first trade.

Regardless of the number of indicators we are able to assign to all different levels of the market there will still always only be one thing that is certain about the markets, that is there is no certainty in the market. Using all types of indicators and strategies we can better predict the outcome of a certain stock over some given time frame. Keywords "better predict." Since we cannot ACCURATELY predict the market movements, it is essential that we keep all of our eggs out of the same basket. This way we are not fooled by the great looking basket that unknowingly has the weakest bottom.

It is important to understand that when trading the most important thing is to preserve your capital. The only real successful traders are the ones that continue to be able to trade day after day and are not wiped out by series unfortunate, unlikely, improbable, or whatever else you may call them, events.

How to create YOUR personal strategy

There are more than a plethora of risk management strategies that fit many different traders' personalities in different ways. This being said, I will focus on a percentage strategy for a few specific reasons, although, many different strategies for risk management exist. This being said, for this trading system to be profitable, it is more important for you to have a risk management strategy firmly set in place than to use the specific strategy that I am going to explain.

As stated above, the most important reason to have a risk management strategy is the fact that, in theory, it will keep you from losing all of your trading money and give you the ability to trade another day. This being said, the basis of any risk management strategy is that it will allow you to risk more as you make more money, yet limit your risks if you are having a losing streak. The easiest way to do this is to say a percent of daily risk you are willing to accept that is based off the daily beginning account balance.

There are essentially two different ways to use the percent strategy. That is you can set a percent that you are willing to risk per trade, or set an amount where you call it quits for the day if you lose that much. Personally, I like to stick with the percent risk per trade. This way if you happen to break a rule, which is easier than it sounds, it will hopefully be limited to a smaller portion of your total account balance.

On the next page I have included a chart with the equation I use when determining risk per trade. The higher risk at lower account balance is explained by the fact that it is still possible to make higher profits with a lower balance, you just need to risk more of your total capital. Also, I have included the chart used to derive this equation to help you better visualize your risk. Remember, you do not have to use these exact risk equations when starting your own trading. Each person has different a different appetite for risk which may be higher or lower than mine. When first starting out, it is advisable to only trade with one contract per position in order to become familiar with the trading before attempting to risk more.

Risk Limits

Balance	% Risk	$ Risk		
$1,500	10%	150		
$3,000	9%	270		
$5,000	7.50%	375		
$10,000	5%	500		
$50,000	3.75%	1875		
$100,000	2.50%	2500		

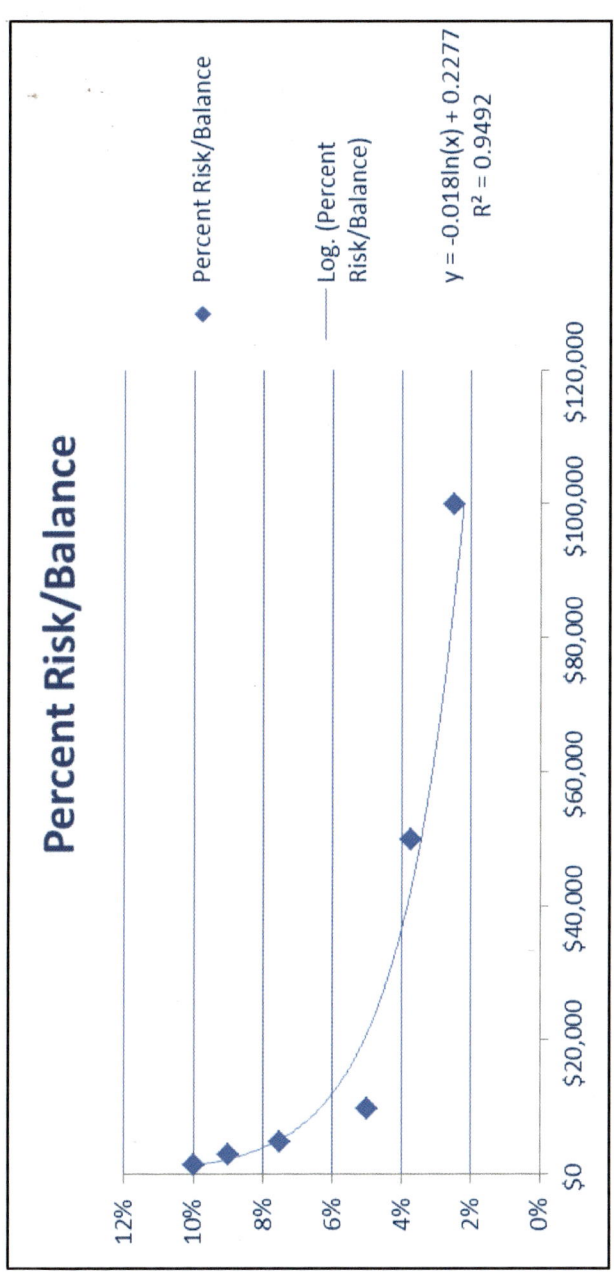

Risk Management Wrap-Up

As simple as implementing a risk management strategy sounds, not implementing one is the primary reason traders fail. When you do implement your own risk management strategy into your trading it is also as important to make sure you stick with it and follow all of its rules, otherwise you might as well not implement it at all and stop trading before you give all your money away.

Finding High Probability Trades

This section will be dedicated to the methods which will help your portfolio see gains instead of losses. When it comes to binary option trading you will be faced with many trades that often need different methods in order to make them profitable. Throughout this section I will explain in detail how to apply each method and when to apply them.

Understanding Binary Options

Whether you are trading stocks, currency, commodities or options you will eventually learn that different parts of the day coincide with different amounts of volatility in the market. Often this doesn't apply to investors so it isn't something frequently discussed in market literature. On the other hand, when trading binary options, being able to predict volatility becomes one of the most essential tools for your ability to make profits.

Traders are often faced with a huge problem when they are trading. If the market doesn't make any relatively large moves in your favor while you hold a position, then you stand to make very little if any profits. Fortunately when trading binary options you can make just as large profits when there is low volatility as you can when there high volatility in the market. Not to mention, one can even use a strategy that bets on NON-volatility.

When determining whether or not to trade a position one will be faced with many variables. These include the underlying instruments position, whether to go long or short on the position, the option price, the time of expiration, the volume, and many other indicators that can be derived from the former. Fortunately, when looking at binary options you are given a huge hint to your probabilities on any given trade.

Using the Binaries Price

A huge break has been given to traders at the Nadex exchange. At expiration, the binaries either settle at 0 or 100. Before the expiration the option trades anywhere within that range, effectively creating a rough probability of whether or not it will pay out at expiration. For example, if the option is trading at $90 per contract, there is roughly a 90% chance of it paying out the $100 at expiry, expiring "in the money." Conversely, if the option is trading at $10, there is only a rough 10% chance that it expires "in the money."

This revelation about binary options will become extraordinarily useful when trading. Although, it is important that these rough probabilities are not taken for more than they are worth, since many other factors are essential in making a high probability trade. For instance, an option could be trading at $70 with what seems like a 70% chance of being in the money, but it is important to know the history of this option as well. If the option has been somewhat volatile and oscillating between $40 and $70 for most of the relevant time frame it would not be advisable to buy this option as its real probability of ending in the money is most likely less than $70. In another example, if the option has been oscillating between $20 and $60, it may be advisable to sell at the $60 price.

Using the Underlying Chart

Each option sold on Nadex has an underlying financial instrument. For example, the EUR/USD options are based on the EUR/USD currency pair. A list of the underlying indicators for each type of option can be found here (https://www.nadex.com/trade/markets.html). The importance of knowing these underlying instruments is very important. First, you are going to want to have a real time data feed for whichever option you decide to trade (discussed in real time data section). You are then going to want to become familiar with its chart and use your chart reading skills to speculate on the direction and volatility of the market.

The prices of the binary derivatives are directly related to the price of the underlying instrument. Therefore, using your knowledge of reading charts, either candle stick, bar or whatever chart type you may use, to exploit and profit from the changes in the derivative price. The idea is that using the underlying indicator it is possible to better pick entry and exit points of the options. It is important to note that an exit point is not always necessary. For example, if you enter a position and the underlying indicator jumps high over the strike price with no indication of a reversal, than you may want to hold on to the option until expiration for maximum profits. On the other hand, if there is a large swing but signs of a reversal are showing, the best idea would be to realize your profits before possibly losing what has already been made.

Using chart indicators from an underlying instrument of the option is the most basic way to explain a good binary option strategy, although, it is not the bulk of your profitable weapons.

Basic Swing Trades

The most basic type of swing trade that can be performed with binary options starts with analyzing charts. You will be looking for indications that the market is preparing to make a "swing" in a certain direction. These indications may include a doji candlestick symbol, volume indicator, or many other indicators that are described in the learning of technical analysis. When one of these is found, you will want to find the aligning binary option contract that you can enter while risking ~$75. Therefore, when long, you will buy a contract for $75: when short, sell a contract for $25.

These are fairly basic trades that should in end up being profitable. Further in the reading we will learn how to hedge our bets to add security and more profitability to our trading.

Hedge to Protect Capital

The bulk of your strategy that will keep you profitable in trading binary options is the ability to hedge your bets. There are many strategies that can be used to accomplish this. Some binary hedging strategies are designed for specific trading environments, while others can be used in many. This section will explain the different environments you will encounter and the hedging strategies that will best accompany them.

When deciding how to hedge your trades you will first be faced with two options, will you be trading a period of volatility or a period of consolidation? As explained in the previous section, it is possible to be profitable even when the market is "consolidating," or has low volatility. This being said, be sure to keep in consideration the market as a whole when deciding which to trade. If the market is consolidating, your individual trading instrument is less likely to be volatile; therefore it would be a bad decision to trade volatility.

Volatility

When trading volatility it is important to be extra cautious. Since you have an expiration time on these contracts, it is important that your predicted volatility happens before that time. The easiest way to do this is to save the volatility trades for times where volatility can be predicted down to a certain minute, such as before a major market announcement. The markets will often make large swings after a jobs report, interest rate announcement by the fed, or when the president speaks about the economy.

There are very few instances when trading binary options that it is advisable to buy contracts for less than $40 or sell them for more than $60, but before these major market announcements it could be. It is possible to invest in two opposite direction contracts during these volatile times and still profit as long as one of them expires in the money. This is because you can enter contracts for a much lower price than the expiration value before these announcements.

For example, you can take $50 to buy a contract at $25 before a major announcement, as well as sell one of the same instruments contracts for $75. After the announcement, as long as one of the contracts expired in the money, you will end up with $100. That is a return of 100% on a strategic trade.

If you are able to predict the markets direction correctly after the major announcement, it is possible to realize extraordinary returns over short amounts of time. If a contract is entered for only $5 before the announcement and expires in the money, the realized return ends up being 2000%. Although, it should understood that it is extremely difficult to make correct market predictions during major announcements and that less risky trades should be made in order to maximize your likelihood of being profitable.

Consolidation

Certain times of the day are often associated with certain market characteristics. For instance, an afternoon session with no major announcements would typically be associated with less volatility. This would be an opportune time to make some trades using a consolidation hedge strategy.

To begin putting together this hedge you will first need to determine a range that the financial instrument should trade in. You will then sell contracts that strike above this range and buy contracts that strike below it. This way you can create a range which you are in the money for both. Plus, if you are unfortunate enough to go out of that high paying range, than at least one will still pay and help to pad your losses.

A Consolidation Trade

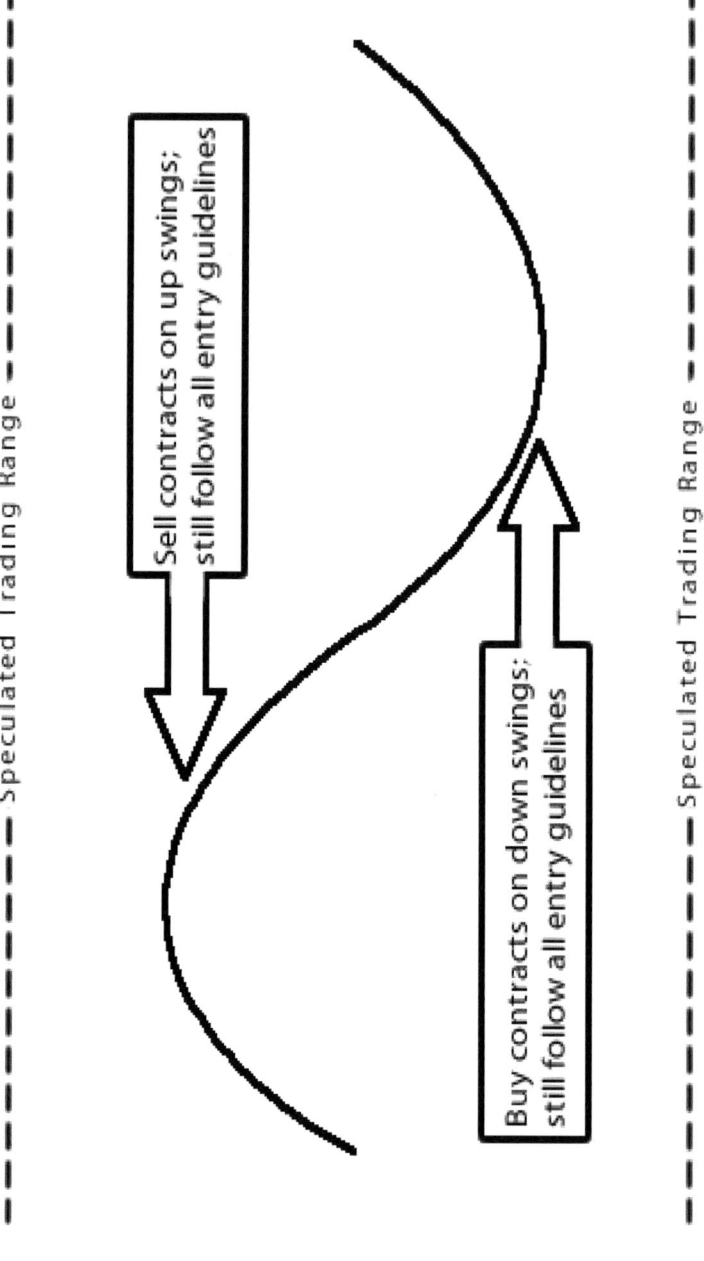

Protection

As you can see, hedging to protect your trade is very simple when working with binary options. When it comes to protecting the start of a good trade the same is true. With any position, you can short a different contract with higher strike price whenever the market makes an overextended up swing. Conversely, a long trade when the market makes an overextended down swing. Therefore you can utilize the benefits of the "range" strategy for a consolidation hedge even when trading volatility.

Each time you decide to make a trade opposite to your previous trades it is important to check the charts technical analysis again. Not every market swing is ideal to make a protection hedge bet. Therefore it is important to determine whether a swing is due to irrelevant noise in the market or something that can change the direction of the market instrument.

Additional Techniques

There is not one, exact, way to consistently make worthwhile profits in the market. Every instrument in the financial world can be traded many different ways with varying results. This section will enlighten any trader with different methods which I found help increase your winning odds when trading binary options.

- Watch out for market announcements
  - o Be aware of all major announcements before beginning a trading day
  - o When trading a day with a major announcement, be sure to trade volatility around the announcement time
- The market often consolidates around lunch time
- ALWAYS check for large trends on different time period charts
  - o You don't want to trade against a major downtrend just because your 1 minute chart has a breakout
- "Trade to trade well, not to make money"
  - o Great advice from one of the first trading books I read
- Be attentive to sudden market changes, getting distracted can cause a lot of damage
- Write out your own plan

- o You should focus on creating a plan more than any other aspect in this guide.

TRADING PLAN

WRITTEN BY BRIAN PETRO

*This is an actual trading plan I created when beginning my career as a binary options trader. It is to be used as a guide to create your own plan, as each individual needs to mold their own plan to their specific trading style. All statements marked with an asterisk (*) denote a place in the trading plan where it is imperative that you evaluate your own system and write it down in your own personal trading plan.

Contents

Mission Statement

The focus of this trading plan is to set out rules and guidelines to follow while trading any type of financial security, with an emphasis on derivatives, specifically binary options.

This plan will layout strategies for trading but will emphasize risk management as the most important instrument for preserving, as well as building, capital.

*This is a very simple mission statement that, at the time, I felt covered all major aspects of what I wanted to do. That is, that I wanted to make money trading binary options.

Trading Goals

Daily

- Create and utilize a stop loss for every trade

Weekly

- Have a higher balance than the previous week
  - Compensation depends on this

Monthly

Yearly

*This is another section that is very important to personalize. These goals can be monetarily specific or broad and based on primarily on your goals of trading well. Regardless of your goals, I find it is very important to write them down in order to reach them the fastest.

Risk Management Guidelines

- Always determine max loss before trading

*When creating this section for myself I had very little to draw out. Personally, I found it most important to always be aware of your risk in order to prevent large losses. This allows you to better determine your risk versus reward. All risk management plans you make should be laid out in your trading plan before you begin trading.

Nadex Trading Strategies

The following strategies are to be used as the only guidelines for entering a position in the Nadex Exchange. All strategies in this document are required to be thoroughly reviewed and researched before being added and/or used in actual trading practices.

This section will include a list of guidelines to follow that apply to every trade and may or may not be indications to enter or exit a position. The next section will be guidelines intended for use before entering a trade, followed by guidelines for exiting a trade.

All of these guidelines should be considered equally as important and used as references before entering any position.

*This section is devoted to understanding what trades I would determine are trades worth making. This way I have a guideline to keep me from making trades that have low probability of paying out. Many of the rules described can be used to keep your trading plan profitable, but it is also very important to adjust your own guidelines to your specific trading style. No two styles should be the same as they should be made in order to counteract the specific emotions of the trader.

Important Guidelines to Follow

> - Trade with the trend
> - Always use the risk equation
> - Never add to a losing position; i.e.,
>   - Never average down
>   - Create a stop for every trade
>   - Obey all stops
> - Preserving capital is the goal
> - Trade volatility before noon
> - Trade stability after noon
> - Record every trade on spreadsheet

Entering a Position

- When entering a long position, option must be valued greater than 50
- When shorting a position, option value must be less than 50
- When entering a reversal, confirm the reversal over at least three different time periods

Exiting a Position

- Do not exit early, but move up stop losses

Compensation

Compensation will be calculated as 10% of the difference between the current week and the previous week given:

- ➢ The difference is positive
- ➢ The difference is less than $2500

If the difference is positive but greater than $2500, compensation will be:

- ➢ 10% of $2500, in addition to;
- ➢ X% of the remainder

If the difference is negative, no compensation will be realized for the week.

Funds may be freely transferred between the designated business account and any desired brokerage account, but funds being transferred to any personal account must abide by these rules.

All compensation calculations will be made between Friday at 5pm and Sunday at 5pm.

*Compensation is a section that will be completely personalized to your needs. Even though your style of compensation may be completely different, it is important that you still create a compensation plan. This way you will have a plan for how you actually get paid as well as how you reinvest your funds. Having a compensation plan that you stick to will be an essential tool to your trading success.

Printed in Great Britain
by Amazon.co.uk, Ltd.,
Marston Gate.

Printed in Great Britain
by Amazon.co.uk, Ltd.,
Marston Gate.